Protect Our Planet

Global Warming

Angela Royston

www.heinemann.co.uk/library

Visit our website to find out more information about Heinemann Library books.

To order:
- ☎ Phone 44 (0) 1865 888066
- 🗎 Send a fax to 44 (0) 1865 314091
- 💻 Visit the Heinemann Bookshop at www.heinemann.co.uk/library to browse our catalogue and order online.

First published in Great Britain by Heinemann Library, Halley Court, Jordan Hill, Oxford OX2 8EJ, part of Harcourt Education. Heinemann is a registered trademark of Harcourt Education Ltd.

Editorial: Sian Smith and Cassie Mayer
Design: Joanna Hinton-Malivoire
Picture research: Melissa Allison, Fiona Orbell and Erica Martin
Production: Duncan Gilbert
Printed and bound in China by South China Printing Co. Ltd.

ISBN 978 0 4310 8474 9
12 11 10 09 08
10 9 8 7 6 5 4 3 2 1

British Library Cataloguing in Publication Data
Royston, Angela
 Global warming. - (Protect our planet)
 1. Global warming - Juvenile literature
 2. Environmental protection - Juvenile literature
 I. Title
 363.7'3874

Acknowledgements
The publishers would like to thank the following for permission to reproduce photographs: © Alamy p.12 (Medio Images); © Corbis RF p.21; © Digital Stock p.19; © Digital Vision p.17; © Ecoscene p.25 right (Eva Miessler); © Getty Images pp.13 (AFP), 4, 16 (Photodisc); © NaturePL p.27 (Arco Reinhard); © Panos pp.9 (Alex Smalles), 8 (Dieter Telemans), 28 (Jocelyn Carlin), 11 (Karen Robinson); © Pearson Education Ltd p.25 left (Gareth Boden); © Photolibrary pp.5 (Daniel Morrison), 14 (Josephine Schiele), 24 (Spence Inqa); © Punchstock p.20 (Fancy); © REUTERS p.29 (Fabrizio Bensch); © Science Photo Library p.7 (Simon Fraser); © Still Pictures pp.22 (Hardy Haenel), 18 (Hartmut Schwarzbach, argus), 23 (Jochen Tack, Das Fotoarchiv), 26 (Martin Bond)

Cover photograph of melting icebergs reproduced with permission of © Corbis (Paul Souders).

Every effort has been made to contact copyright holders of any material reproduced in this book. Any omissions will be rectified in subsequent printings if notice is given to the publishers.

Contents

Any words appearing in the text in bold, **like this**, are explained in the Glossary.

What is the Earth?

The Earth is one of the **planets** that circles around the Sun. The Earth has land, oceans, rivers, and air. It is the only planet where scientists know for sure that living things exist.

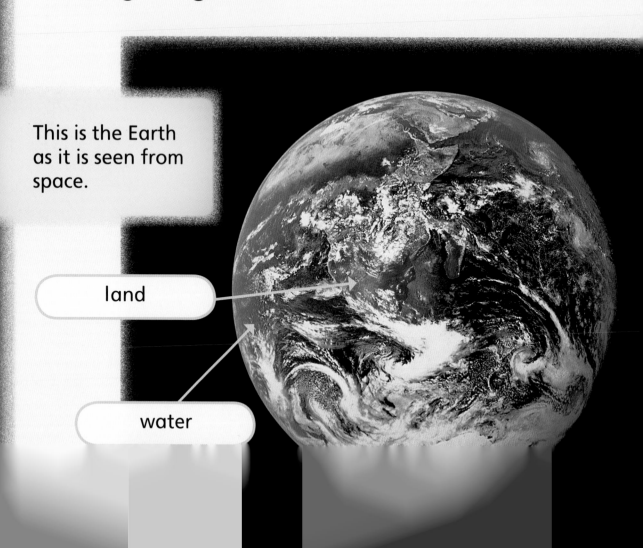

This is the Earth as it is seen from space.

land

water

The Sun shines on the Earth and gives it light and heat. The Earth gets the right amount of heat for millions of different plants and animals to live here.

What is global warming?

The temperature of the Earth has risen a small amount during the last 100 years. This is called **global warming**.

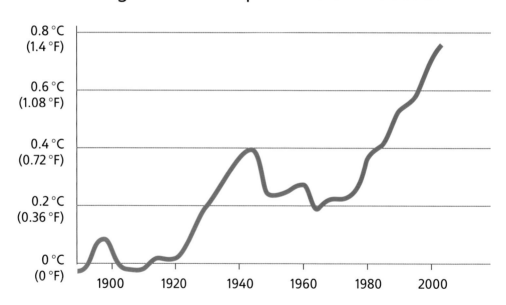

Changes in the temperature of the Earth

This graph shows a rise in the average temperature of the Earth.

Most of the rise in the temperature of the Earth has happened in the last few years.

This is a weather thermometer. It measures the temperature of the air.

Some parts of the Earth are always hotter or colder than other parts. Global warming is making most places on Earth a little bit warmer.

More extreme weather

Global warming is changing the weather in many areas of the world. For example, in some places the summer is now hotter than it used to be. And in many places it rains much less than it used to.

This dry land used to be a golf course. It was covered with grass.

KEEP OFF GRASS

Strong winds can damage buildings and cause flooding.

Hurricanes are fierce storms with very strong winds. In some places hurricanes are getting stronger.

Bigger deserts

Deserts are places that get almost no rain. Very few plants, animals, or people can live in a desert. **Global warming** is making deserts larger.

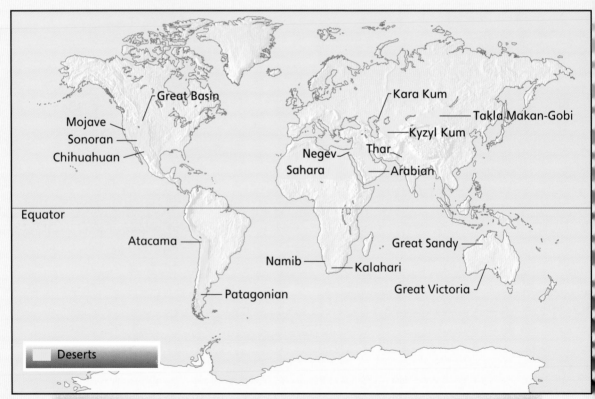

The world's deserts are shown here in yellow. Global warming is causing more land to become desert.

This land in Kenya is becoming too dry for these goats to live on.

More land is becoming too dry for plants to grow. When this happens, there is nothing for animals to eat. The people who live on this land have to move to somewhere else.

Melting ice

The **Arctic** and **Antarctic** are the coldest parts of the Earth. They are covered with very thick ice all year round. **Global warming** is causing some of this ice to melt.

If the temperature of the Earth continues to rise, more and more cities will be flooded.

As the ice melts, extra water runs into the oceans. This means that the level of the sea is slowly rising. If the sea rises too much, it will flood cities, towns, and land near the coast.

What causes global warming?

The air is a mixture of gases. One of the gases is **carbon dioxide**. Carbon dioxide and some other gases in the air are called **greenhouse gases**.

A greenhouse is warm inside because it traps the Sun's heat.

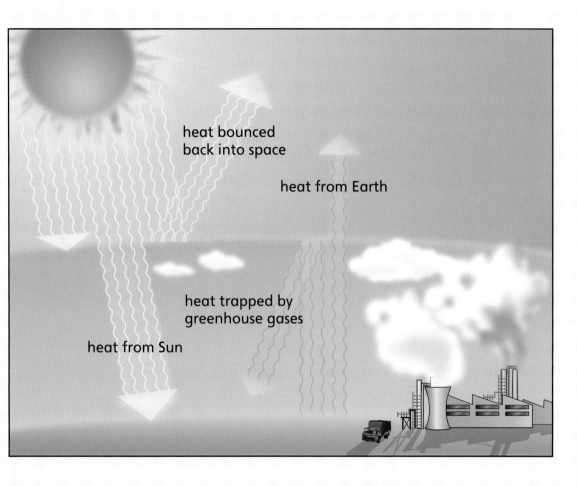

heat bounced
back into space

heat from Earth

heat trapped by
greenhouse gases

heat from Sun

Greenhouse gases trap some of the
Sun's heat. The amount of carbon
dioxide and other greenhouses gases in
the air is increasing. This is causing the
Earth to become warmer.

Where does carbon dioxide come from?

Global warming is caused by extra **carbon dioxide** in the air. Almost all of this extra carbon dioxide is made by people when they burn **oil**, coal, and **natural gas**.

This car burns petrol to make it go. When petrol burns it makes carbon dioxide.

This is a power station. When it burns coal to make electricity, it also makes carbon dioxide.

People use oil to make petrol for cars and lorries, and **fuel** for aeroplanes. **Power stations** burn coal, oil, and natural gas to make **electricity**. People use electricity to light their buildings and to make televisions and other machines work.

17

Can global warming be stopped?

People can slow down **global warming** by burning less coal, **oil**, and **natural gas**. Scientists are inventing new **fuels** and engines that do not make so much **carbon dioxide**. These are called **low-carbon** fuels and engines.

This bus uses a fuel that makes no carbon dioxide.

Wind turbines make electricity when their blades turn in the wind.

Scientists have invented ways of making **electricity** without burning coal, oil, and natural gas. One way is to use the power of the wind to make electricity. **Wind turbines** can make electricity. They do not create carbon dioxide.

19

Low-carbon electricity

Some **power stations** use flowing water to make **electricity**. A **dam** is built across a valley to make a lake. Some of the water from the lake flows through the dam and the power station. This kind of power station does not make **carbon dioxide**.

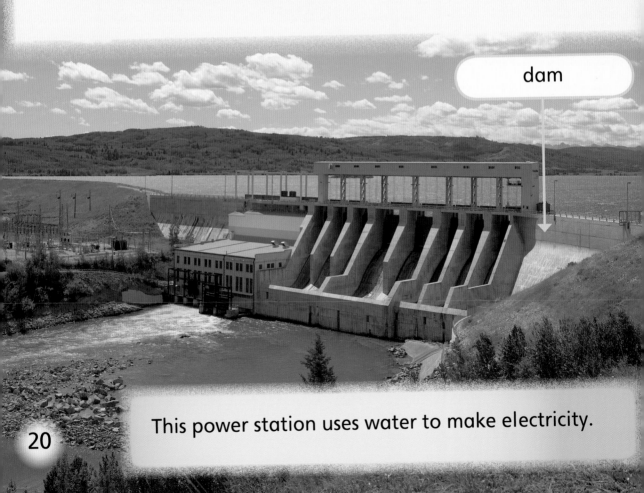

dam

This power station uses water to make electricity.

The Sun can be used to make electricity. Many mirrors guide the Sun's rays onto one spot. Here a liquid becomes very hot and the heat is used to make electricity.

Low-carbon transport

Scientists are designing buses, cars, and vans that make little or no **carbon dioxide**. Some use **biofuels**, which are made from plants. Others use **electric motors**. The **electricity** they need can be made without making carbon dioxide.

These plants can be used to make biofuel.

Most vehicles still burn **fuel** made from **oil**.
Aeroplanes and cars make the most carbon
dioxide. People should travel by train or bus
whenever they can. Walking and cycling
are the best ways to travel short distances,
because they make no carbon dioxide.

Low-carbon homes

Scientists are finding ways to make buildings **low-carbon**. Solar power panels on the roof use sunlight to make **electricity** and they make no **carbon dioxide**. The panels work during the day, but not at night.

solar panels

regular light bulb

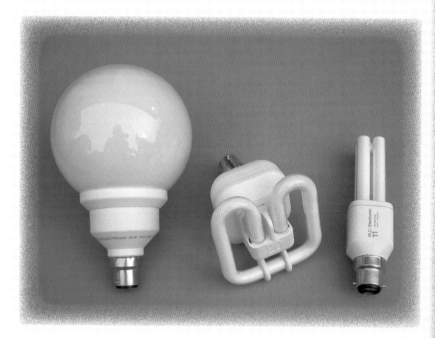

low-energy light bulbs

Homes can be designed so that they do not use very much electricity or gas for heating and cooling. People can also save energy by using low-energy light bulbs.

Low-carbon living

This house is called Earthship. It can be found in New Mexico, in the United States. The people who live here do not create any **carbon dioxide**.

Earthship was built using old rubber tyres, mud, and drink cans.

Growing your own food means that lorries, ships, and aeroplanes have to carry less food to shops.

Earthship uses only a small amount of **electricity**. The electricity is made by solar panels and a small **wind turbine**. The people who live in Earthship grow most of the food they eat.

The bigger picture

Carbon dioxide created in one part of the world causes **global warming** all around the world. The United States and China make the most carbon dioxide.

Tuvalu is an island in the South Pacific. It is becoming flooded because of global warming.

These people want countries to agree to cut the amount of carbon dioxide they create.

All countries need to work together to cut the amount of carbon dioxide they are creating. If they do so, they can help to stop the worst problems of global warming.

Glossary

Antarctic land and sea around the South Pole where it is very cold all year round

Arctic land and ocean around the North Pole where it is very cold all year round

biofuel fuel made from plants that vehicles can use to make them move

carbon dioxide one of the gases in the air. Carbon dioxide is a greenhouse gas.

dam wall that blocks a river to make a lake

desert area of dry land that gets very little rain

electricity form of energy used to make machines work

electric motor engine that uses electricity to make something work

fuel substance such as gas, wood, or coal that is burned to give heat, light, or power

global warming rise in temperature of the surface of the Earth, including the land, sea, and air

greenhouse gas gas in the air that traps some of the Sun's heat and so makes the Earth warmer

low-carbon making very little or no carbon dioxide

natural gas gas that is found under the ground. It is burned in homes to make heat.

oil liquid found under the ground. It is burned in vehicles and in power stations.

planet huge lump of rock or a large mass of gas and liquid that circles around a star

power station building where electricity is made

wind turbine machine that makes electricity using blades that spin in the wind

Find out more

Books to read

Reduce, Reuse, Recycle: Energy, Alexandra Fix (Heinemann Library, 2007)

The Dangers of Global Warming: Why are the ice caps melting? Anne Rockwell; Paul Meisel, (Collins, 2006)

Websites to visit

www.epa.gov/climatechange/kids/
This is the website of the United States Environmental Protection Agency. It gives information about global warming.

tiki.oneworld.net/global–warming/climate–home.html
Tiki the penguin tells you how global warming is affecting his home.

Index